This
## David Bennett Book
belongs to

ALICE

Findlay

First published in paperback in 1993
by David Bennett Books Ltd,
94 Victoria Street, St Albans,
Herts, AL1 3TG.
First published in hardback in 1991
by Kingfisher Books

Consultant: Dr Julian Hector

BRITISH LIBRARY CATALOGUING IN PUBLICATION DATA
A catalogue record for this book is available
from the British Library.
ISBN  1 85602 054 1

Typesetting by Type City
Production by Imago
Printed in Hong Kong

# I am a
# Duck

Written by
# Linda Bygrave

Illustrated by
# Louise Voce

David Bennett Books

I am a duck.
I like to live near water.

Like all birds, I have feathers
covering my body.
They keep me warm and dry.

You can often see me in parks.
I am usually by the water
because I love to swim.

You have probably heard
the sound I make.  What is it?
That's right!  "Quack, quack!"

I have short legs and
big webbed feet.

This means that I have skin
between my toes.  Look!

Because my legs are so short,
I am not very good at walking.
I waddle from side to side.

But I am a wonderful swimmer.
I use my webbed feet to paddle
along in the water.

I use my wings for flying.
I can even take off from water.
Here I go!

I can land on water too.
I use my webbed feet like brakes.
They slow me down as I land.

I like to keep myself very clean.
I use my beak to clean my feathers,
just like you use a brush or comb.

I spread a special oil on my feathers,
which helps to keep them dry.
The oil comes from near my tail.

I mostly feed on plants in the water.
Sometimes people feed me bread.

To reach the plants under the water,
I tip myself up like this.

I am a mummy duck.
Over there is a daddy duck.
He is called a drake.

His feathers are a different colour
from mine.  He is showing them to me
because he wants us to have babies.

It is early spring and I have made
a nest of leaves and grass.
I have ten beautiful eggs in my nest.

I have spread soft plants
around the inside of the nest
to make it warm and cosy.

I sit on my eggs for about a month.
Then my ducklings start to hatch out.
Look! Aren't they tiny?

My ducklings are covered
in soft, fluffy feathers called down.
They are very hungry.

My ducklings can swim as soon
as we go into the water.
They follow me in a neat little line.

I say, "Quack, quack!"
They say, "Cheep, cheep!"
This way, we can always find each other.

I must watch my ducklings carefully
and stop big fish and birds
from getting too close to them.

In about six weeks, my ducklings will
be able to fly.  It has been a busy day
and it is time for us to rest.  Goodbye!

Other David Bennett paperbacks you will enjoy . . .

**I am a Duck** *Linda Bygrave • Louise Voce*  *ISBN 1 85602 054 1*

**I am a Frog** *Linda Bygrave • Louise Voce*  *ISBN 1 85602 051 7*

**I am a Butterfly** *Linda Bygrave • Louise Voce*  *ISBN 1 85602 052 5*

**I am a Rabbit** *Linda Bygrave • Louise Voce*  *ISBN 1 85602 053 3*

As featured on BBC TV's *Playdays*. The perfect nature library for the very young.

**If Dinosaurs Came To Town** *Dom Mansell*  *ISBN 1 85602 044 4*

'. . . combines detailed pictures and evocative language with inviting tit-bits of science' *The Independent*

**The Monster Book of ABC Sounds** *Alan Snow*  *ISBN 1 85602 041 X*

An ABC of sounds, which follows a riotous game of hide-and-seek between a group of rats and monsters.

**Inside Big Machines** *Arlene Blanchard • Tony Wells*  *ISBN 1 85602 043 6.*

A fascinating look inside some of the world's biggest machines.

**Teddy Bear, Teddy Bear** *Carol Lawson*  *ISBN 1 85602 040 1*

A beautifully illustrated version of the classic children's activity rhyme.

**One Cow Moo Moo!** *David Bennett • Andy Cooke*  *ISBN 1 85602 042 8*

As featured on BBC TV's *Over The Moon*. A farmyard romp through numbers from one to ten.